ELECTRICITY
AND
MAGNETISM

Steve Parker

HODDER
Wayland

an imprint of Hodder Children's Books

SCIENCE FACT FILES

THE EARTH'S RESOURCES
ELECTRICITY AND MAGNETISM
FORCES AND MOTION
LIGHT AND SOUND
THE SOLAR SYSTEM
WEATHER

Produced by Roger Coote Publishing
Gissing's Farm, Fressingfield
Suffolk IP21 5SH

First published in 2000 by Hodder Wayland
An imprint of Hodder Children's Books
This paperback edition published in 2001
Text copyright © 2000 Hodder Wayland
Volume copyright © 2000 Hodder Wayland

Title page picture: Inside a television studio

Design and typesetting Victoria Webb
Commissioning Editor Lisa Edwards
Editor Steve Setford
Picture Researcher Lynda Lines
Illustrator Alex Pang

We are grateful to the following for permission to produce photographs: Digital
Stock 9 top (Marty Snyderman), 16 bottom left (Bud Freund), 39 right; Digital
Vision *front cover background*, *front cover top right*, 18/19, 23, 29 bottom, 30
bottom, 34, 41, 42 top, 43 bottom. Science Photo Library 8 (Doug Martin), 10
bottom (Peter Menzel), 12 bottom (David Parker), 13 (Kent Wood), 14 bottom
(David Nunuk), 18 top and 18 bottom, 19 bottom (Phillippe Plailly/Eurelios), 20
(Charles D. Winters), 21 middle (Richard Megna), 26 bottom (Alex Bartel), 29 top
(Francoise Sauze), 31 (John Mead), 33 top (Hank Morgan), 35 top (James Holmes),
37 bottom (Simon Fraser), 38 top (BSIP VEM), 38 bottom (Malcolm Fielding, The
BOC Group plc), 41 top (BSIP S&I), 41 bottom (Will and Deni McIntyre), 42 middle
(David Scharf); The Stock Market 5, 9 bottom (Jeff Zaruba), 25 bottom; Tony Stone
17 (Marc Dolphin), 25 top (Marc Pokempner), 36 (Mary Kate Denny); Roger Vlitos
front cover bottom right.

The statistics given in this book are the most up to date available at
the time of going to press.

Printed in Hong Kong by Wing King Tong

A CIP catalogue record for this book is available from the British Library
ISBN 07500 2720 7

Hodder Children's Books, a division of Hodder Headline Ltd
338 Euston Road, London NW1 3BH

CONTENTS

The words that are explained in the glossary are printed in **bold** the first time they are mentioned in the text.

INTRODUCTION

Using a computer, vacuum-cleaning the carpet, navigating through a jungle, having a scan in hospital – so many of the things we do rely on the amazing properties of electricity or magnetism.

What are electricity and magnetism?

Electricity is a form of energy. Energy, in turn, is the ability to make things happen, to cause activity or to do work. The energy of electricity is based on the movement of tiny particles known as **electrons**. Electricity is a very convenient form of energy, because it can be made to travel along wires to wherever it is needed. It can also be converted into other forms of energy, such as movement, heat, light and sound.

Robot car-welders use electrical energy to produce heat, light, sound and motion.

HISTORY FILE

MYSTERIOUS ATTRACTION

• About 2,550 years ago in Ancient Greece, the philosopher Thales described how if a lump of amber – hardened plant sap or resin – is rubbed with a cloth, it will attract dust and feathers. Today, we know that this attraction is caused by electricity.

• Some 150 years later in Ancient China, the 'Yellow Emperor' Huang-Ti is said to have used a long, slim lump of lodestone rock to navigate and lead his troops into battle against invaders. Resting on a wooden float in a bowl of water, the lodestone slice always turned to point north–south. This was an early type of magnetic compass.

• The mysterious and invisible attracting powers of magnetism and electricity were confused with each other for hundreds of years, until the scientific advances of the 18th century.

Magnetism is an invisible force with the power to attract or repel certain substances – mainly those containing the metal iron. A simple use of magnetism is a note-holder that 'sticks' to the refrigerator. A more complex use is in a magnetometer, a device that detects deposits of metal ores under the Earth's surface (see page 23).

Electricity and magnetism in nature

Electricity and magnetism may be the basis of much modern science and technology, but they also occur naturally in the world around us. Lightning, for example, is caused by electricity, while our own bodies are constantly producing millions of tiny electrical nerve impulses 24-hours a day. Magnetism is also naturally occurring: the rock lodestone, which contains iron, is magnetic, as is the Earth itself.

Linked forces

Electricity and magnetism are so closely linked that one can produce the other. For example, electricity flowing through a wire will produce an area of magnetism around the wire, while a magnet moving near a wire will produce electricity within the wire. Together, electricity and magnetism make up the force called electromagnetism. This is one of the four basic or fundamental forces that hold the Universe together. The others are gravity, the force that attracts all objects to one another, and the strong and weak nuclear forces, which are only found within the centres of **atoms**.

An electromagnetic world

Electromagnetism shapes our lives in many different ways, especially through the relatively new science of electronics. It provides many people with comfortable homes, labour-saving devices, automated factories and advanced medical techniques. It also allows us travel around the world and communicate instantly with people on the other side of the globe.

Sensors on a shark's nose can detect tiny electrical pulses in the water given out by the muscles of the shark's prey.

This TV studio is crammed with screens, which use both electricity and magnetism.

ELECTRICITY AND ATOMS

To understand electricity, it helps to know something about atoms – the tiny particles from which everything in the Universe is made. Atoms themselves contain even tinier particles called protons, neutrons and electrons. The centre, or **nucleus**, of an atom consists of protons and neutrons bound tightly together. The nucleus is surrounded by a cloud of moving electrons.

Nucleus is a tight bundle of particles called protons and neutrons

Particles called electrons orbit the nucleus in layers, or shells

Inner electron shell

Outer electron shell

An atom's central part, or nucleus, is surrounded by fast-moving electrons.

Electrical charge

Protons and electrons carry small amounts, or charges, of electricity. There are two types of **charge**: positive (+) and negative (–). A proton carries a positive charge, while an electron carries a negative charge. A neutron has no charge at all. Atoms normally contain equal numbers of protons and electrons, so their positive and negative charges balance each other. This means that the atoms and the materials they form are usually neutral – in other words, they have no overall electrical charge.

How objects become charged

If two materials are rubbed together, electrons may be transferred from one to the other, upsetting the balance of charge that keeps the materials neutral. For example, when you rub a plastic ruler with a woollen duster, some electrons are dislodged from atoms in the ruler and transferred to atoms in the duster. The ruler now has fewer electrons than protons, so it becomes positively charged. The duster has more electrons than protons, so it becomes negatively charged.

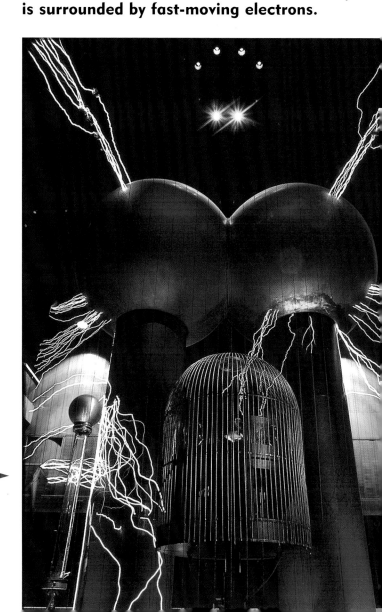

In scientific research, huge machines like this Van der Graaf generator build up billions of volts of electrical charge.

FUN WITH CHARGES

• If you rub a balloon against your sweater, the balloon becomes negatively charged and the sweater gains a positive charge. The two charges attract, so the balloon clings to the sweater when you let go of it.

• When you brush your hair with a plastic comb, the comb gains a negative charge, while your hair becomes positively charged.

The positive charges on the individual strands of hair repel each other, making your hairs stick up.

• You can use your negatively charged balloon or comb to pick up tiny pieces of paper. The negative charge induces a positive charge on the surface or the paper, so the paper sticks to the balloon or comb.

Attraction, repulsion and induction

Electrical charges exert forces on each other. Unlike charges (positive and negative) attract each other. Like charges (two positives or two negatives) repel, which means that they try to push each other apart. Charged objects can also produce, or 'induce', charges in neutral objects when they are held close to them. A negatively charged object pushes electrons away from the surface of a neutral object, giving the surface a positive charge. On the other hand, a positively charged object attracts more electrons to the neutral object's surface, giving the surface a negative charge. This is called **electrostatic induction**.

FACT FILE

ELECTRICAL CHARGE

• Electrical charge is measured in units called coulombs (C). One coulomb is equivalent to the charge on 6 million million million electrons.

• Electrical charge can be stored in a device called a capacitor. The charge can be released in a rush when it is required.

• Capacitance is the amount of charge that a capacitor can store for a certain strength, or voltage, of electricity. Capacitance is measured in units called farads.

• Many types of electrical equipment use capacitors, including camera flashes, tuning knobs on radios, and the devices that control the supply of electricity to electronic devices such as computers.

Unlike charges attract, so balls with positive and negative charges will pull together.

Like charges repel, so two negatively charged balls will push each other apart.

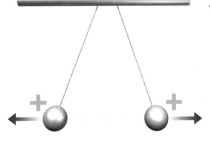

Two positively charged balls will repel each other.

STATIC ELECTRICITY

When an object becomes electrically charged, the positive or negative charges space themselves out over the object's surface and wait for the chance to move. Electricity in the form of charges that do not flow steadily is called **static electricity**.

Using static electricity

The forces of attraction and repulsion between electrical charges makes static electricity useful in industry, especially when a surface needs to be coated with small droplets or particles. In a car factory, for example, a paint-spraying machine gives the same charge to all the tiny paint droplets it sprays over a car body. The droplets repel each other and space out equally over the surface of the car to form an even coating of paint, rather than clumping together. The car body is given the opposite charge to attract the drops and reduce waste.

Many photocopiers work by static electricity. Inside a photocopier, an image of the document to be copied is projected onto a large drum. Static electric charges form on the parts of the drum where the image is dark. These attract fine black

particles of toner powder, which have the opposite charge and form a visible image on the drum's surface. The drum transfers the toner to electrically charged paper and it is fixed in place by heat.

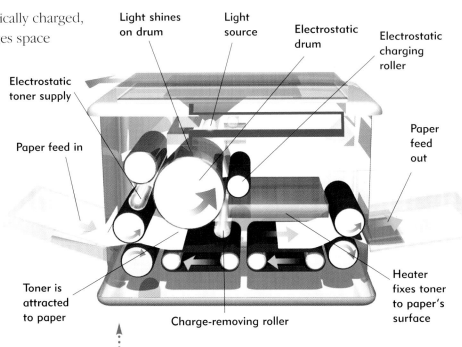

Light shines on drum · Light source · Electrostatic drum · Electrostatic charging roller · Electrostatic toner supply · Paper feed in · Paper feed out · Toner is attracted to paper · Charge-removing roller · Heater fixes toner to paper's surface

A photocopier uses electrostatic charge to attract toner (powder) onto the paper.

The droplets in the fine mist of paint from a spray- gun are all given the same charge as they come out of the nozzle. This forces them to repel each other and so spread out evenly, instead of collecting into larger blobs.

Static discharge

Sometimes, a charge builds up and becomes so numerous and powerful that there is a **static discharge** – a sudden rush of charge that evens out or corrects the imbalance. The electrons always go from a negative to a positive area. A lightning bolt is perhaps the most dramatic example of a static discharge.

What causes lightning?

Swirling air currents inside thunderclouds make ice crystals and water droplets collide with such force that electrons are transferred between atoms, generating static electric charges within the clouds. The imbalance of charge builds up until a huge spark called a lightning bolt leaps between the clouds to even out the imbalance. This is called sheet lightning. The lightning bolt is so fast and powerful that it heats the air instantly, producing light and sound as well.

TEST FILE

HOW FAR AWAY IS THE STORM?

Lightning and thunder happen at the same time. But light travels at 300,000 km/s, while sound travels nearly a million times slower, at only 330 m/s. So we see lightning almost as soon as it occurs, but hear the thunder a short time later.

You can work out the distance to the lightning by the time difference between the flash and the 'boom'. Every second is about 330 m (one-third of a km). So if the gap between the lightning and thunder is 6 seconds, the storm is about 2 km away.

The charged clouds can also induce positive charges in the ground below, so the lightning sometimes discharges to the ground instead of between clouds. This is called forked lightning.

Lightning bolts are giant discharges of electricity that produce light and sound.

FACT FILE

LIGHTNING!

• Lightning heats air to 30,000 °C, five times hotter than the Sun's surface!
• The sudden intense heat makes the air expand faster than the speed of sound. This breaks the sound barrier and produces a 'sonic boom', which we hear as the clap of thunder.
• A medium-sized lightning bolt contains enough electricity to supply a large town with power for more than one year.
• At any time of day or night, about 2,000 thunderstorms are raging around the world, producing around 100 flashes of lightning every second.

CURRENT ELECTRICITY

A lightning bolt is a spectacular example of electrical charge on the move, although it is not a great deal of use to us. But when charge can be made to flow as a continuous stream of electrons – an **electric current** – it becomes an invaluable source of power for homes and industries.

How does charge flow?

Imagine a line of people, each holding a tennis ball. Each person gives the tennis ball to the person in front, and takes the tennis ball from the person behind. In this way the tennis balls move steadily along, while the people stay still. When an electric current flows through a metal wire, a similar process happens. The metal atoms are like the line of people, while electrons are like the tennis balls. The electrons move from one atom to the next, but the atoms stay where they are.

Plastic insulating case

Electrical cells

Switch makes and breaks the circuit

Screw-cap end with spring connector

Brass connecting strip

Reflector

Switching on a torch completes a circuit, so that a current can flow out of the cells, through the bulb and back into the cells.

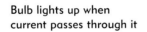

Bulb lights up when current passes through it

Powerful electric currents flow along cables held high on pylons for safety.

Conductors and insulators

Charge can only flow steadily through materials called **conductors**. In a conductor, electrons are bound only loosely to their atoms, so they can move easily through the material. Most metals and liquids are good conductors. Conductors cannot be charged with static electricity, because the charge always flows freely away.

Other materials, called **insulators**, block the flow of current. The electrons in an insulator cannot move through the material because they are held tightly to their atoms. Most natural fibres (such as wool and cotton), artificial fibres (such as nylon and acrylic), plastics, wood, card, paper, glass and pottery are all good insulators, as is the air around us. Electrical wires and cables are coated with plastic insulator to prevent current from flowing where it is not needed, avoiding danger or wasting electricity.

Some materials, such as silicon and germanium, are unusual in that they conduct electricity only under certain conditions. For this reason, they are known as **semiconductors**. They are used in electronic devices to control current.

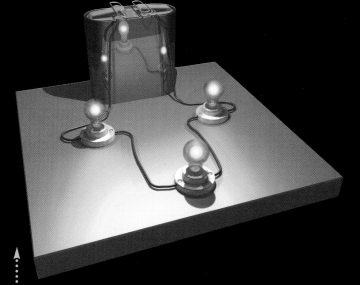

In a series circuit the electric current flows from its source, such as a cell or battery, through each device or component in turn and then back to the source.

In a parallel circuit each device or component has its own path for electricity and does not rely on any others. The current flows through them all at the same time.

CIRCUITS AND CURRENTS

There are two main types of circuit.

• Series circuit: components are connected like links in a chain. The electric current passes through each of the components one after the other, and its strength, or voltage, is shared between them all. If one component fails, the circuit is broken and none of the components works.

• Parallel circuit: each component is connected to a separate branch of the circuit. The current passes through all of them at the same time, along parallel paths, and they each receive the full voltage. If one component fails, the circuit is not broken and the other components continue to work.

There are also two main ways in which electricity can flow around a circuit.

• **Direct Current (DC)**: in direct current, electricity flows continuously in the same direction. Electrical cells and batteries in torches and similar devices make DC.

• **Alternating Current (AC)**: in an alternating current, electricity flows first one way around a circuit, and then the other, changing direction many times each second. The electricity supply to your home is AC. It changes its direction 50 times each second.

Making a circuit

For a current to flow, the electrons need a continuous path to follow, called a **circuit**. The basis of this path is usually a loop of insulated copper wire, because the metal copper is a good conductor. The electrons also need a 'push' to get them moving around through the wire. This push is called **electromotive force (emf)** and it comes from devices such as batteries and **generators**, which kick-start the flow of electrons around the circuit.

Components

Bulbs, motors and other electrical devices that can be connected to a circuit to make use of the current are known as components. A switch is a component that completes or breaks a circuit. When you turn on a switch, for example, it closes a gap in the circuit with a strip of conducting material, allowing the current to flow. When the switch is turned off, the gap is opened again. This breaks the circuit and stops the current's flow, because the air that fills the gap is an insulator.

CELLS AND BATTERIES

An **electrical cell** is a convenient, transportable source of electric current. People often refer to cells as batteries, but a battery is really a series of cells linked together. A typical cell contains a conducting chemical called **electrolyte** and two rods or plates called **electrodes**. Each electrode is made of a different conducting material (such as copper, zinc, or carbon) and forms or joins to one of the battery's two terminals, through which current leaves and returns to the cell.

When the cell is connected into a circuit, a chemical reaction occurs between the electrolyte and the electrodes, stripping electrons from their atoms. The electrons flow out of the cell through the negative terminal. This supply of electrons gives the pushing force – the emf – to start electrons moving all around the circuit, and an electric current flows. Electrons always flow from the negative terminal, around the circuit, and back to the positive terminal.

The increasing use of mobile phones has led to the development of improved rechargeable batteries.

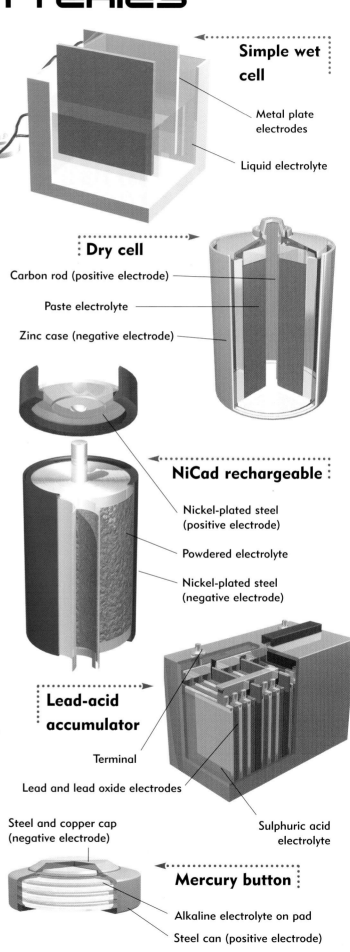

Simple wet cell

Metal plate electrodes

Liquid electrolyte

Dry cell

Carbon rod (positive electrode)

Paste electrolyte

Zinc case (negative electrode)

NiCad rechargeable

Nickel-plated steel (positive electrode)

Powdered electrolyte

Nickel-plated steel (negative electrode)

Lead-acid accumulator

Terminal

Lead and lead oxide electrodes

Sulphuric acid electrolyte

Steel and copper cap (negative electrode)

Mercury button

Alkaline electrolyte on pad

Steel can (positive electrode)

Most people power their personal stereos with primary dry cells. Although they are compact and efficient, these cells eventually lose their power and have to be thrown away.

A longer-lasting type of dry cell is the alkaline cell, which uses potassium hydroxide as the electrolyte. Tiny dry cells called button cells are used when a larger cell would be too bulky and inconvenient, such as in a hearing aid or wristwatch. There are several different types, including the mercury oxide cell, which has electrodes of mercury oxide and zinc.

NiCads are small rechargeable dry cells that contain nickel and cadmium. They are often used in toys, cordless power tools and phones, and portable computers. NiCad cells can be recharged from the domestic electricity supply using a suitable charger.

Lead-acid batteries

The battery found inside a car consists of rechargeable wet cells. Its electricity is used to turn the starter motor and get the engine going. The engine then drives a generator that recharges the battery. Car batteries contain sheets of lead and lead oxide, which are the electrodes, hanging in a bath of sulphuric acid, which is the electrolyte.

Primary and secondary cells

Some cells, called primary cells, go 'dead' and lose their power after a while, so they have to be thrown away. This is because the electrodes and electrolyte change as they react together. When the change is complete, the reaction stops and no electricity flows. But other cells, called secondary cells, can be recharged with electricity. Passing an electric current through them reverses the changes that have taken place, so that the electrolyte and electrodes reform and the cell can be used again.

Dry cells

The electrolyte in dry cells is in the form of a powder or paste. (Cells with a liquid electrolyte are called wet cells.) Dry cells are used in torches, personal stereos, radios, and similar devices. One of the most common types is the zinc-carbon cell. Its electrolyte is a paste of ammonium chloride. The positive electrode is a carbon rod in the middle, while the negative electrode is the cell's zinc metal case. This type of cell is sometimes called a Leclanché cell, after its inventor George Leclanché (1839–1882).

HISTORY FILE

THE FIRST BATTERY
In 1800, Italian physicist Alessandro Volta (1745–1827) made the first battery from a pile of alternating metal discs of zinc and copper, with paper discs soaked in salt solution or weak acid between each of the metal discs. It was the first source of steadily flowing electrical current, and opened up a whole new area of scientific experiments, discoveries and inventions.

MEASURING ELECTRICITY

It is vital that we can describe, measure and monitor the electricity in a circuit, not only for our own safety, but also to check that the parts and components of the circuit are suitable, working properly and not at risk of damage. Because of this, scientists have developed their own words, units and measurements for electricity. Many of the units are named after scientists and inventors who contributed to the study of electricity and energy.

Alessandro Volta

Volts (V)

The strength of an electric current is expressed in units called volts. Volts measure the electromotive force (emf) that pushes electrons round the circuit. A typical torch cell produces a current of 1.5 volts, and a car battery 12 volts. The domestic electricity supply is 110 or 220 volts, and high-power cables on tall pylons carry 400,000 volts or more. The volt is named after the Italian physicist Alessandro Volta (1745–1827), who made the first battery.

Georg Ohm

Amperes (A)

The rate at which current flows through a circuit is measured in amperes or amps. A current of 1 amp means that 6 million million million electrons flow past a certain point in the circuit every second. A typical cell-powered electrical device, such as a torch, uses only a fraction of an amp. An electric kettle uses about four amps. The amp is named after the French scientist André-Marie Ampère (1775–1836), who studied the links between electricity and magnetism.

Ohms (Ω)

The ohm is the unit that measures **resistance** – the way in which materials oppose or slow down the flow of current. Even the best conductors have a small amount of resistance, perhaps just a few ohms. A light bulb glows because its filament – the thin coil of wire inside it – has a resistance of several hundred ohms. As electricity pushes hard though the filament to overcome the high resistance, it makes the filament very hot, so it shines brightly. The ohm is named after the German scientist Georg Ohm (1789–1854), who studied resistance.

FACT FILE

USEFUL EQUATIONS

The different units of electricity are linked by the following simple equations, which help electrical engineers and circuit designers to calculate how many amps, volts, ohms and watts should be present in any part of a circuit.

• Voltage (volts) equals current (amps) multiplied by resistance (ohms): $V = A \times \Omega$. This is called Ohm's law.

• Power (watts) equals voltage (volts) multiplied by current (amps): $W = V \times A$.

Engineers need to be able to measure electricity to check or repair circuits and equipment.

Scientists are researching materials called superconductors, which have virtually no resistance.

Watts (W)

The watt is the unit of power, which is the amount of energy used per second. The power of any machine is measured in watts, from electrical devices to car and rocket engines. A typical domestic light bulb uses about 60 or 100 watts. A hair drier uses 1,000 watts, or one kilowatt (kW).

The watt is named after the Scottish engineer James Watt (1736–1819). This is not because of his work on electricity, because he did none! It is because of his development of the steam engine, which was the main source of power from the late 1700s to the late 1800s.

MAGNETISM

agnetism is an invisible force possessed by objects called magnets. It can attract or repel certain objects and materials, especially those containing iron. Magnets come in many different shapes – from bars, horseshoes and discs to rings and balls – and in a whole range of sizes. Every magnet has a **magnetic field**, an area around the magnet in which the magnetism exerts its power. The magnetic field gets weaker farther away from the magnet. In a bar-shaped magnet, the field is strongest at each end, or pole, of the magnet. The field loops around the magnet from pole to pole.

TEST FILE

EXPERIMENTS WITH MAGNETS

1. See a magnetic field
Put a magnet under a piece of paper. Shake iron filings over the paper and tap it gently. The magnet pulls the filings into a pattern that shows the shape of its magnetic field. The lines you see are called lines of magnetic force.

2. Find out which materials are magnetic
Hold a magnet next to various objects. Can you feel any pull or attraction? If you cannot, the object is made of non-magnetic material. If there is a pull, the object is magnetic and probably contains iron.

3. Make a magnet
Bend a steel paper-clip straight. Stroke it along its length with one pole of a magnet, always in the same direction, lifting the magnet well clear between strokes (see opposite). The magnet makes all the domains in the clip face the same direction, turning it into a magnet.

4. Destroy a magnet
Take an old magnet you no longer want, and bang it hard lots of times. This jumbles up the domains and destroys the magnetism (see opposite). Heating a magnet will also destroy its magnetism.

A magnet pulls steel items towards itself.

Magnetic materials

Materials that exert magnetism or are affected by it are said to be magnetic. They include the metals iron, cobalt, and nickel, and other materials in which these metals are found. Steel, for example, is a mixture of metals and is magnetic because it is about 90 per cent iron. The rock lodestone is also magnetic, because it naturally contains iron.

Other metals and other materials are not affected by magnetism, so they are non-magnetic. However, a magnetic field can pass through some non-magnetic materials, such as paper, wood, glass and air.

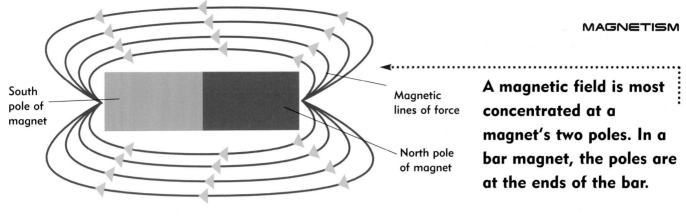

South pole of magnet

Magnetic lines of force

North pole of magnet

A magnetic field is most concentrated at a magnet's two poles. In a bar magnet, the poles are at the ends of the bar.

North and south

Because the Earth has an iron core, it too exerts magnetism. It has a magnetic field and two magnetic poles, which are found near the Earth's geographical North and South Poles. If a bar magnet is allowed to swing freely from a thread, it aligns itself with the Earth's magnetic field, and always ends up with one pole pointing north and the other pointing south. This is why a magnet's two poles are called north and south (or north-seeking and south-seeking).

When two bar magnets are placed end to end, the poles of the magnets will either snap together or spring apart. A magnet's north and south poles behave like the positive and negative charges in electricity. Unlike poles (north and south) attract, while like poles (south and south, or north and north) repel each other.

What causes magnetism?

Magnetism, like electricity, is based on the structure of atoms. Each atom has negatively charged electrons travelling round a positively charged nucleus. It also has a magnetic field, caused by the way that the electrons spin around as they orbit the nucleus at high speed, and by the way the nucleus itself spins.

Atoms form into tiny regions of magnetism called **domains**, each with a north and south pole. In a magnet, the domains neatly line up, with all their north poles pointing the same way. Their effects combine to give a strong magnetism. In a non-magnet, the domains are not lined up, so they cancel each other and there is no overall magnetism.

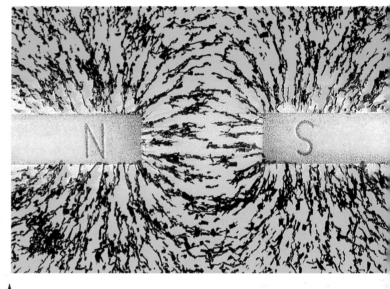

Magnetic lines of force are normally invisible, but iron filings (tiny flakes) line up with them and enable them to be seen.

Stroking an iron bar with a magnet aligns the domains and turns it into a magnet. Hitting the bar destroys its magnetism.

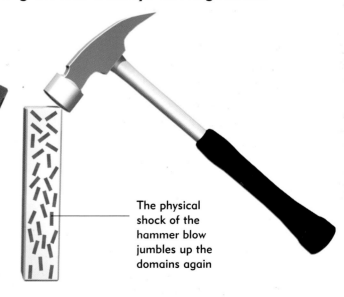

Domains point in all directions

Domains line up, and bar becomes a magnet

The physical shock of the hammer blow jumbles up the domains again

USING MAGNETISM

Magnets have many simple uses around the home, such as a sewing magnet that can pick up scattered steel pins and needles. Many can-openers have a magnet that holds a food can steady as it is opened, while a screwdriver's steel shaft may be magnetized to hold the screw on the tip of its blade and make screwing it in easier.

Some burglar alarms use magnets fixed to doors to detect intruders. With the door closed, the magnet attracts a piece of metal on the frame, pulling it forward so that it touches electrical contacts and completes a circuit. When the door opens, the metal piece springs back, breaking the circuit and triggering the alarm.

Finding your way

A magnetic compass is a useful navigation tool, because it always points north-south. Inside the compass is a free-swinging needle mounted on a pivot. The needle is actually a long, thin magnet, so it is attracted by the Earth's magnetic field. It always comes to rest pointing towards the Earth's north and south magnetic poles. However, navigators must also take into account the fact that the Earth's magnetic poles are slightly offset from the geographical ones.

Maglev trains lack wheels. They are held above the track by repulsion between magnets in the track and on the train.

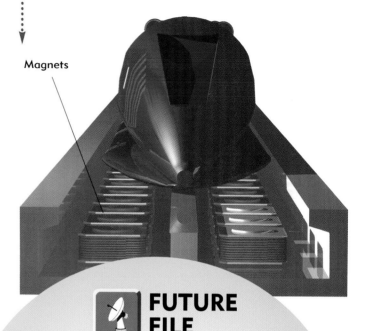

Magnets

🛰 FUTURE FILE

FLOATING TRAINS
Engineers are developing experimental trains that use the repelling forces of magnets to travel along a track. These trains are known as magnetic levitation (maglev) trains. The train and the track contain powerful magnets arranged so their like poles face each other. The like poles repel, lifting the train above the track so that it 'floats on air'. This eliminates friction and enables the train to travel fast using little fuel.

Forces of attraction and repulsion propel the train along the track

Huge mining machines dig out iron ore, located using magnetic instruments.

Locating minerals

The Earth's magnetic field varies slightly across its surface, and these variations are often signs that there are valuable mineral deposits below ground. For example, thick layers of iron ore (iron-containing rocks) bend or distort the lines of magnetic force. Scientists use very sensitive instruments called magnetometers to detect these variations and locate the iron ore.

Magnetic bearings

Bearings are devices that reduce rubbing or friction – the force that opposes motion – between moving parts such as wheels and axles. Because friction occurs where moving parts touch, magnetism can be used to eliminate friction by pushing the moving surfaces apart. For example, if a wheel hub and an axle shaft are magnetized, they will repel each other so that the wheel hub can rotate around the axle without touching it, removing the problem of friction.

Storing information

Magnetism is also used to store information on audio and video tapes, and on the discs used in computers and some cameras. The information can represent words, numbers, sounds, pictures and computer data. It is put into coded form and recorded as patterns of magnetism on the surface of the tape or disc, which has a metal coating of iron oxide or chromium oxide. The dark stripes on credit cards and security passes contain similar patterns of magnetism that carry coded information.

FACT FILE

MAGNETIC FIELD STRENGTHS
The strength or intensity of a magnetic field, known as magnetic flux, is measured in units called webers (w). The strength of magnetism in a certain area (such as a square metre), known as magnetic flux density, is measured in units called teslas (T).
• Average strength of Earth's magnetic field at the surface: 0.000,05 teslas.
• A note-holding fridge magnet: 0.02 teslas.
• Fairly powerful permanent magnet, as in a hi-fi loudspeaker: 0.1–0.2 teslas.
• Very powerful magnet: 0.5 teslas.
• Surface of a neutron star (the corpse of a dead star), which is one of the most powerful known magnetic fields in the Universe: 100 million teslas.

ELECTROMAGNETISM

When electricity flows along a wire, it produces a magnetic field around the wire. The field's lines of magnetic force go around the wire, like a series of tubes one inside the other. This is known as the electromagnetic effect. As in a magnet, the magnetism is caused by the spinning, moving electrons in the wire.

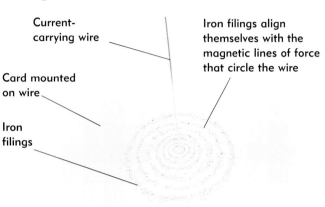

Current-carrying wire

Card mounted on wire

Iron filings

Iron filings align themselves with the magnetic lines of force that circle the wire

If you fix a piece of card around a current carrying wire and sprinkle iron filings over the card, the filings align themselves with the wire's magnetic field.

The magnetism can be strengthened and concentrated by winding the wire into a long coil, called a solenoid. The more turns there are in the coil, the more powerful the magnetic field. Wrapping the coil around an iron bar makes the field even stronger. The iron bar then becomes a magnet, but only while the electricity flows. The result is a device called an electromagnet, whose magnetism can be switched on and off, so that you can have a magnet whenever you need it. And by making the electric current stronger or weaker, the magnetic field can be made stronger or weaker. This makes electromagnets more useful than ordinary, permanent magnets.

TEST FILE

MAKE YOUR OWN ELECTROMAGNET
• Wrap a length of insulated copper wire tightly around a large iron or steel bolt or nail, keeping the coils as close together as possible. If necessary, use sticky tape to hold the coils in place.
• Make sure there is plenty of wire left over at either end once you have coiled it round the nail.
• Attach a metal paper clip to each end of the wire, and slip the paper clips over the terminals of a 4.5- or 9-volt battery.
• Test your electromagnet by placing dressmaking pins close to it. The pins should cling to the electromagnet.
• Disconnect the wire from the cell and the magnetism ceases.
• Using paper clips, drawing pins and a small piece of soft wood, you can add a switch to your circuit by copying the arrangement in the picture below.

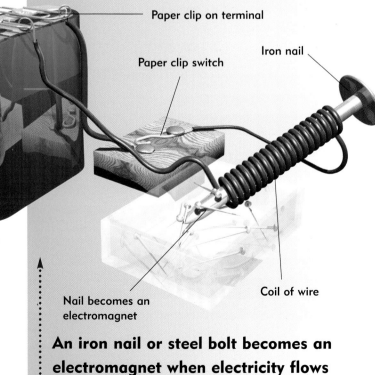

Paper clip on terminal

Iron nail

Paper clip switch

Coil of wire

Nail becomes an electromagnet

An iron nail or steel bolt becomes an electromagnet when electricity flows through a wire coil wrapped around it.

Magnetism makes electricity

The electromagnetic effect can also work the other way around. For example, when a wire moves within the field of a magnet, it causes an electric current to flow along the wire. Similarly, a moving magnetic field will produce a current in a stationary wire. A current can also be produced when the magnet and the wire are stationary if the magnetic field changes in strength. This is called **electromagnetic induction**.

The pick-ups on an electric guitar rely on electromagnetic induction.

HISTORY FILE

AN AMAZING DISCOVERY
Hans Christian Oersted (1777–1851) was a professor of physics at Copenhagen University. During a lecture in 1820, he noticed that when he passed a strong electric current through a wire on his desk, the needle of a nearby compass flicked or deflected slightly, so that it no longer pointed north–south. He realized that the electric current had produced a magnetic field around the wire. Almost by chance Oersted had discovered the electromagnetic effect.

Play it again

Electromagnetic induction has many uses. Play an electric guitar on its own, and it is extremely quiet. But plug it into an amplifier and speaker, and it can be very loud! Below the guitar strings is a device called a pick-up, which consists of a coil of wire wound around rod-shaped magnets called pole pieces. When the strings are plucked they vibrate within the magnetic fields of the pole pieces. The vibrations cause the magnetic fields to vary in strength, producing a varying current in the wire by electromagnetic induction. The current is strengthened by an amplifier and changed into sound by a loudspeaker.

Metal detectors at security checks often use electromagnetism to detect iron-containing objects such as guns.

USING ELECTROMAGNETISM

Electromagnets have a great advantage over ordinary or permanent magnets because they can be controlled easily, turned on and off, and made more or less powerful by changing the strength of the current.

Electromagnetic recycling

A large electromagnet can lift great weights, even cars. Big electromagnets are used at recycling centres and scrapyards to lift and separate the ferrous (iron-containing) metals from other discarded materials. For example, the electromagnet could pick up all the food or 'tin' cans (which are made mainly of iron-based steel) and leave behind the drink cans (which are aluminium).

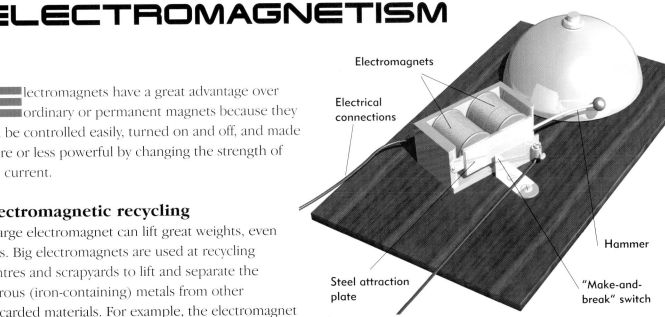

Electromagnets

Electrical connections

Steel attraction plate

Hammer

"Make-and-break" switch

An electric bell uses electromagnets to pull the hammer against the bell.

Electromagnetism on your doorstep

The button of an electric doorbell is a switch. Pressing the button allows current to flow through an electromagnet inside the doorbell mechanism. The magnetic field produced by the electromagnet pulls a metal hammer forward so that it strikes the bell. As it does so, it temporarily breaks the circuit. The magnetic field disappears and the hammer springs back to its original position. This reforms the circuit so that the current flows again and the hammer strikes the bell once more. This sequence of events happens over and over again, giving the continual 'ring' until you take your finger off the button.

Security-door lock

The lock of a remote-controlled security door uses a special arrangement of a solenoid and an iron bar. The iron bar, which forms the door latch, is not fixed inside the coil of the solenoid but is able to slide to and fro. A spring mechanism ensures that the door is normally locked, with the metal latch pulled across into the door frame. When someone calls, you first speak to them on an intercom to find out who they are. If you want to let them in, you press a button, which sends a current through the solenoid coil.

This industrial electromagnet attracts only iron-containing scrap metal, which can then be melted down and recycled.

The magnetism produced by the coil pulls the latch out of the frame and unlocks the door. When the button is released, the electricity stops, and the latch springs back to lock the door again.

Sound to electricity

Sound travels as waves of vibrations. A microphone changes sound waves into electrical signals. It contains a wire coil that sits within the field of a permanent magnet. The coil is attached to a thin cone of material (often plastic or metal) called a diaphragm, which vibrates when sound waves strike it. This causes the coil to move within the magnetic field and induces a fluctuating electric current to flow through the coil. The fluctuations in the current mirror the vibrations in the sound waves. The signals can then be recorded or turned back into sound by a loudspeaker.

FUTURE FILE

SATELLITE LAUNCH BY MAGNETS
Launching a satellite into space by rocket is hugely expensive. Another way to launch rockets might be to use electromagnets. The satellite could be put into a streamlined magnetic case, then into a giant tube hundreds of metres long. The tube would have many ring-shaped electromagnets along its length. Switching the electromagnets on and off in quick succession would pull the satellite in its case along the tube, faster and faster. The satellite would eventually be hurled out of the end of the tube, like a huge bullet from a giant gun, high into space.

Telephones transmit sound using microphones and loudspeakers

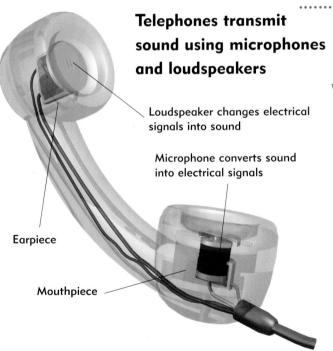

Loudspeaker changes electrical signals into sound

Microphone converts sound into electrical signals

Earpiece

Mouthpiece

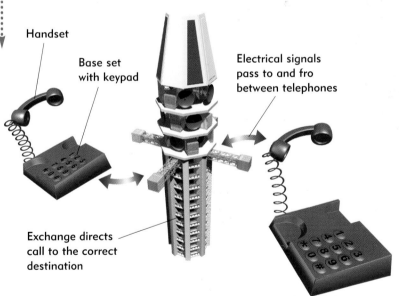

Handset

Base set with keypad

Electrical signals pass to and fro between telephones

Exchange directs call to the correct destination

Electricity to sound

A loudspeaker works in the opposite way to a microphone. Fluctuating electrical signals from a radio, television or music system pass through a coil of wire, which is attached to a diaphragm and sits within the field of a large permanent magnet. When electricity flows through the coil, it becomes an electromagnet. Its magnetic field pushes and pulls against the field of the permanent magnet,

making the coil vibrate. The vibrating coil causes the diaphragm to vibrate and produce sound waves.

A telephone handset contains both a microphone and a loudspeaker. The microphone changes the sound of your voice into electrical signals. The signals are sent along the telephone line to an exchange, from where they are sent on again and changed back into sound by a loudspeaker in the handset of the person receiving your call.

ELECTRIC MOTORS

One of the most important uses for electromagnetism is the **electric motor**. This is a device that changes electrical energy into rotary (round-and-round) motion, which can be harnessed to drive machinery.

A simple electric motor consists of a wire coil mounted on a shaft and sitting between the north and south poles of a permanent magnet. A pair of carbon connectors called brushes feed electricity to the coil. When a current flows through the coil it becomes an electromagnet, with its own north and south poles. The magnetic fields of the magnet and the coil interact, and the forces of attraction and repulsion between their poles push the coil up on one side so that it makes half a turn. The direction of the current flowing through the coil is then reversed. This has the effect of reversing the poles of the coil's magnetic field, so that the coil is pulled down on the other side, completing the turn.

Most motors have several coils mounted on the same shaft and several sets of brush contacts. As the motor spins round, one coil after another is activated, giving a smooth, continuous turning force.

DC motors

The electric motors found in toys, tape players and other equipment are powered by cells and batteries. Because the batteries supply the motor with DC (direct current, see page 15), which only flows one way, the coil would normally stop after the first half-turn. To overcome this problem, a rotating switch called a commutator is attached to the same shaft as the coil. It changes the current's direction every half-turn, ensuring that the coil keeps spinning round and round.

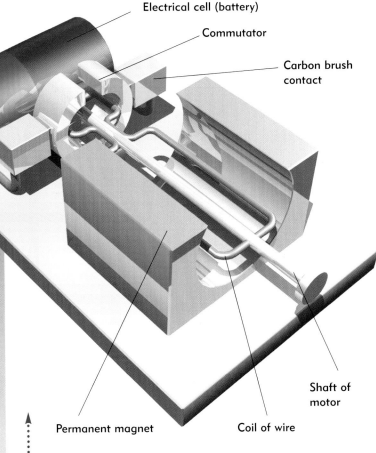

Electrical cell (battery)

Commutator

Carbon brush contact

Shaft of motor

Coil of wire

Permanent magnet

In this simple DC (direct current) electric motor, there is just a single rotating wire coil. Most motors have several coils, each with hundreds of turns.

HISTORY FILE

ADVANCES IN ELECTRIC MOTORS

1821: English scientist Michael Faraday (1791–1867) made a current-carrying wire spin around a magnet. Although it changed electrical energy to rotary motion, it was not a true electric motor.

1831: US scientist and engineer Joseph Henry (1797–1878) made an early practical electric motor.

1870s: Generators in power stations started to produce reliable electricity for domestic and industrial use, and electric motors began to be used more and more in factories, and later homes.

1888: Croatian-American engineer Nikola Tesla (1856–1943) designed the first induction motor. The success of the induction motor was a key factor in AC rather than DC being used for the domestic electricity supplies.

FACT FILE

MOTOR EFFICIENCY

Of all the mechanical devices that convert energy into motion, electric motors are among the most efficient.

• A steam engine changes about 20 per cent of the energy stored in its fuel into movement.

• For a petrol engine, the proportion is about 40 per cent.

• For an electric motor, the proportion is more than 90 per cent.

• The fastest electric-motor-driven trains travel at 515 km/h.

• The fastest electric-motor-driven cars travel at 295 km/h.

High-speed trains have electric motors driving each set of wheels.

AC motors

The electric motors in washing machines, vacuum cleaners and similar appliances are connected to the mains supply, which is AC (alternating current, see page 15). These AC motors do not need a commutator, because, as we have seen, the current is made to change direction many times each second.

Another type of AC motor is the induction motor. It consists of a set of outer coils, called the stator, encircling an inner coil, called the rotor, mounted on a shaft. When electricity flows through the stator, it passes first through one coil, then the next, and so on in quick succession, producing a magnetic field that rapidly rotates. This induces a current to flow through the rotor, so the rotor also becomes an electromagnet. As the stator's magnetic field spins, it 'drags' the rotor around with it.

Most power tools, such as this circular saw, use AC (alternating current) motors.

GENERATING ELECTRICITY

While electric motors change electrical energy into motion, a generator does the opposite. A simple electricity generator has much the same parts as a simple electric motor, with a coil of wire mounted on a shaft between the poles of a permanent magnet. When the coil is made to turn by a mechanical force, the movement of the wire within the magnetic field induces an electric current to flow through the wire. Brushes and wires carry away the electricity.

AC and DC generators

When the turning coil of a generator passes one of the magnet's poles, electrons are pulled through the wire in one direction, but as the coil passes the magnet's opposite pole, the electrons are pulled through the wire in the opposite direction. So the electric current flowing through the coil changes direction twice for every turn of the coil, producing an alternating current. When generating electricity for a mains supply, a generator spins a steady 50 times per second, so the current also changes direction 50 times each second. AC generators are called alternators.

A generator that has a commutator and brushes, like a DC motor, can produce electricity which is DC rather than AC. Although the current that flows through the coil still alternates, the commutator (or another electrical device) constantly reverses the electrical connections to the generator, so that the current that emerges is direct, and only flows one way. This type of generator is used in some vehicles.

Carbon-brush contact

Commutator

Bulb

Wire coil

Permanent magnet

Shaft is turned by mechanical force

A DC (direct current) electrical generator has much the same parts as a DC electric motor (see page 28). The bulb would shine equally well using AC or DC.

A hydro-electric power station has a dam to hold back most of the water. This allows a steady flow even at dry times.

FACT FILE

POWER STATION GIANTS

These are the world's largest power stations of their kind:

• The Itaipu Power Complex is a series of hydro-electric dams and power stations on the Paraná River between Brazil and Paraguay. It is the world's largest electricity producer, with an output of 13,320 million watts. Hydro-electric power stations do not burn fuel so they do not produce polluting fumes or radioactive wastes.

• The biggest nuclear power station is at Zaporizhzhya, Ukraine. It produces 6,000 million watts.

• The largest wind-powered electricity generator is at Oahu, Hawaii. In favourable winds it produces just over 3 million watts.

• The largest solar power station, at Harper Lake in the Mohave Desert, USA, produces 160 million watts.

Many aerogenerators located together at a windy place, such as a moorland or mountain pass, are known as a wind farm.

Large generators, such as those used in power stations, have complex arrangements of coils. Instead of having a spinning coil and a stationary magnet, they may have rotating magnets within stationary coils. Smaller, simpler generators are sometimes called dynamos. They include the bicycle dynamo, an alternator that harnesses the motion of a bicycle wheel to produce electricity for the lights.

Generators in power stations

Inside most power stations, burning fuel or **nuclear reactions** heat water and change it into high-pressure steam. The steam is fed past a turbine, which consists of a set of angled blades mounted on a shaft. The force of the moving steam on the blades makes the turbine spin. The turbine's shaft is connected to the shaft of an electricity generator, so when the turbine spins it provides the mechanical force to drive the generator.

Not all power stations use steam to spin the turbines. In a hydro-electric power station, water flowing down from a dam or waterfall presses on the turbine blades and makes them rotate. A tidal power station is positioned across a river estuary. As the tides come in and go out, the to-and-fro movement of huge volumes of water powers the turbines. An aerogenerator consists of a large, propeller-like turbine attached to a generator and mounted on a tall tower. As the wind blows, moving air forces the propeller round.

Small portable generators are not powered by turbines. Instead, they are usually linked to a petrol engine, whose drive shaft powers the generator. In a diesel-electric train, a diesel engine turns the generator to make electricity, which is then fed to the electric motors that turn the train's wheels.

ELECTRICITY DISTRIBUTION

Electricity from power stations travels along cables to wherever it is needed. Most power-station generators produce AC electricity at the strength of about 22,000 volts. This is too low to be carried efficiently along the cables of power lines. Resistance in the cables changes some of the electricity into heat and wastes energy. Less electricity is lost at higher voltages, so the electricity from the generators is boosted to about 400,000 volts – sometimes even more – to make sure a minimum of energy is lost when it is sent through power cables. This is done by devices called transformers, which change, or transform, the voltage of the electricity.

Transformers

A simple transformer has two coils of wire wound around an iron core. When AC electricity flows through one coil (called the primary coil), it turns the metal core into an electromagnet. The core's magnetic field continually changes strength and direction as the current flows back and forth. This changing field induces AC electricity to flow through the other coil (called the secondary coil). So electrical energy transfers, via magnetism, from one coil to the other.

The flow of electricity around the supply network is constantly checked.

Stepping up the voltage

The size of the voltage in the secondary coil depends on how many turns of wire there are in each coil. When the primary and secondary coils have the same number of turns, the voltage in the two coils is the same. But if the secondary coil has more turns than the primary, the voltage is increased ('stepped up').

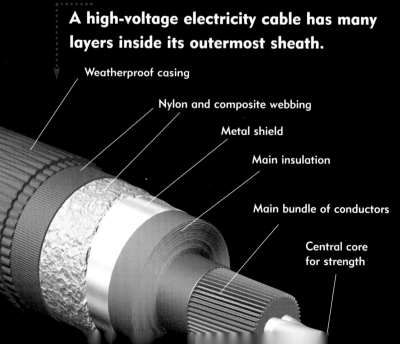

A high-voltage electricity cable has many layers inside its outermost sheath.

- Weatherproof casing
- Nylon and composite webbing
- Metal shield
- Main insulation
- Main bundle of conductors
- Central core for strength

FACT FILE

HOW MANY VOLTS?
- Heavy industrial plants and factories, such as a steel works, need high voltages of about 33,000 volts.
- Light industrial plants, such as a factory for assembling electronic goods, use 11,000 volts.
- Smaller workshops, farms and similar users receive 415 volts.
- The domestic electricity supply is 220 volts.
- For some machines and appliances, such as computers and personal stereos, 220 volts is still far too powerful. So they contain their own step-down transformers that reduce the electricity to 24, 12, 9 or even fewer volts.

This is called a step-up transformer. Twice the number of turns gives twice the voltage, three times the number gives three times the voltage, and so on.

When a step-up transformer raises the voltage of the electricity supply, the current (the number of electrons flowing) falls in proportion. This is because the higher voltage pushes the electrons harder through the cables, so fewer are needed to carry the same amount of electrical power (see equations on page 19). The total electrical power in the primary and secondary coils is much the same.

Stepping down the voltage

When the high-voltage electricity in power cables reaches its destination, the voltage has to be reduced for use in homes, schools, hospitals, offices, factories, and other places. This is done by step-down transformers in electricity substations. A step-down transformer works in the opposite way to a step-up transformer. It has more turns in the primary coil than the secondary, so a smaller voltage but larger current is induced in the secondary coil.

The electricity grid

Power cables link all the different elements of the electricity distribution system – power stations, transformers, substations, and users – into a network called a grid. Just as a road network in a town gives you a variety of routes to reach your destination and avoid traffic jams, the grid gives several alternative routes for electricity to travel to users. This enables it to bypass parts of the system that are faulty or overloaded. If one part of the system needs more electricity than the local power station can supply, electricity can be supplied from power stations in other areas.

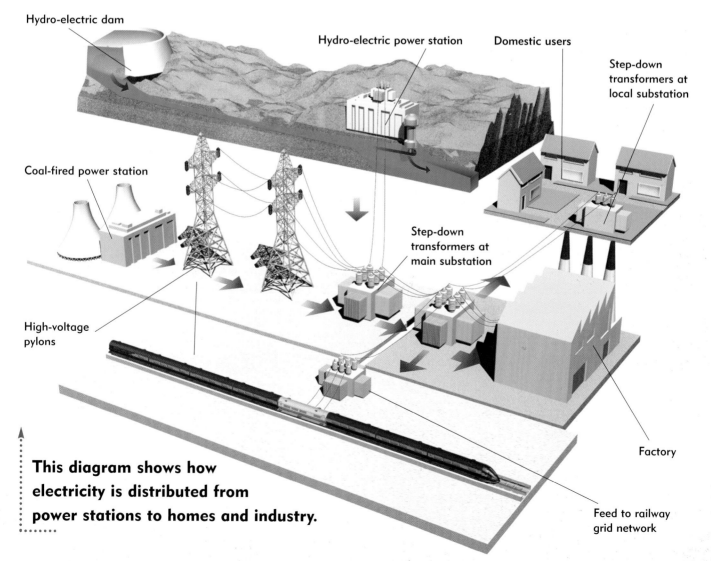

Hydro-electric dam

Hydro-electric power station

Domestic users

Step-down transformers at local substation

Coal-fired power station

Step-down transformers at main substation

High-voltage pylons

Factory

Feed to railway grid network

This diagram shows how electricity is distributed from power stations to homes and industry.

When the electricity bill has to be paid, it seems like a typical home uses a huge amount! But industry uses thousands of times more electrical energy than homes, offices and schools added together.

The most obvious use of electricity in a factory is for lighting, but not surprisingly this usually forms the smallest part of the bill. The next biggest item on the bill after lighting is movement. A modern factory is a maze of machines, and most are driven by electric motors. Conveyor belts, rollers, hoists, drills, lathes, hammers, grinders, mixers, pumps, sprayers, even robot arms – the uses of electric motors are almost endless.

The largest part of a factory's electricity bill is usually heating. This includes heaters to keep people warm, and also processes that use heat to purify, cook, make and shape products. For example, one electric oven in a large bakery, or an electric furnace in a pottery, uses as much electricity as all the homes in a small town.

Apart from providing lighting, heating and power for machinery, electricity is also needed for many industrial processes. One of the most important is **electrolysis**, which uses an electric current to split up complex chemicals into simpler ones.

A steelworks needs huge quantities of electricity to generate enough heat to melt and shape the metal.

How electrolysis works

Many dissolved substances consist of electrically charged particles called **ions**. Ions are atoms that have gained or lost electrons, so they carry positive or negative charges. When the substance is molten or dissolved in a liquid to form a solution, the ions are free to move around. In this state, the substances are called electrolytes.

Two electrodes – a negative one (the cathode) and a positive one (the anode) – are placed in the electrolyte. The electrodes are usually made of metal. An electric current is then passed between the electrodes. This causes the charged ions to move towards the electrode with the opposite charge, since unlike charges attract. For example, when sodium chloride (salt) solution is electrolyzed, the substance splits up as positive sodium ions move to the negative cathode, while negative chloride ions move to the positive anode.

Electrolysis is used to refine (remove impurities from) substances such as sodium and copper.

TEST FILE

NEW SPOONS FOR OLD

If you can obtain some copper sulphate crystals from a chemistry kit or pharmacy, you can electroplate a spoon with copper. (Never eat or drink copper sulphate crystals or solution. Wash your hands after using them.)

• Dissolve the crystals in water in a glass bowl.

• Connect the spoon to the negative terminal of a 4.5- or 9-volt battery using a length of wire.

• Use another wire to connect the battery's positive terminal to a piece of copper plumbing pipe, which forms the other electrode.

• Dip both electrodes into the solution in the bowl.

• Positive copper metal ions are attracted to the negative spoon electrode, and soon cover it all over with a shiny new coppery coating.

Copper transfers from the copper sulphate solution and copper pipe onto the spoon.

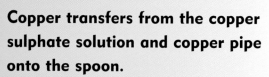

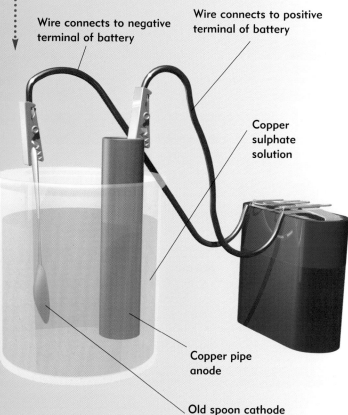

Wire connects to negative terminal of battery

Wire connects to positive terminal of battery

Copper sulphate solution

Copper pipe anode

Old spoon cathode

These electrolysis tanks at a chemical plant produce chlorine gas by splitting up salty water (sodium chloride solution).

Some of the world's biggest electricity-users are aluminium smelting plants, which use electrolysis to obtain aluminium metal from the rock ore bauxite. Bauxite contains the substance aluminium oxide. In the smelting plant, the aluminium is extracted by heating a solution of aluminium oxide to almost 1,000°C and then electrolyzing it.

Electroplating

Electrolysis is used in electroplating, a method of covering or 'plating' an object with a very thin layer of metal. The object to be electroplated is connected into a circuit so that it becomes one of the two electrodes. The electrodes are placed in an electrolyte containing ions of the metal that will form the plating. When current flows through the electrolyte, metal ions are attracted to the object and coat it all over in an even covering. Silver-plated objects, such as jewellery, are given thin coating of silver over a much cheaper metal. Zinc is used to plate steel objects such as cans, cars and buckets, to make them rust-proof.

ELECTRICITY IN THE HOME

Modern homes rely on electricity. Even a central heating system that burns coal, gas or oil has an electric time clock so that it switches on and off at the right times, an electric thermostat to control the temperature and an electric pump to send the water around the radiators. Only during a power cut do we suddenly realize how much we depend on electricity.

The meter and consumer unit

Electricity enters the home via overhead or underground cables from the local substation. These have thick insulation, both for their protection and our own safety. Once in the home, the cables go to a meter that measures how much electricity is used. The cables then pass to a device called a consumer unit. This splits the electricity into several different circuits, such as those for the lights, wall sockets, cooker, immersion heater, central heating and other appliances.

If there is a fault in a circuit, the current may reach dangerous levels, heating wires so much that a fire starts. Because of this, each circuit has its own circuit-breaker or fuse. A circuit-breaker is an electromagnetic switch activated by excessively high current. In the event of a fault, it switches off only its own circuit, leaving the others unaffected. This means that a problem with the hot-water immersion heater does not result in every circuit being switched off and the whole house being plunged into cold and darkness.

Almost every domestic machine, including the dishwasher, relies on electricity.

FACT FILE

HOW MUCH ELECTRICITY DO THEY USE?

To give you an idea of how much electricity is used by electrical appliances, this list shows you how long different household gadgets would run on 1,000 watts (1 kW) of electrical power. The longer they run, the less electricity they use.

Instant shower	8 minutes
Electric double-oven	15 minutes
Electric kettle	30 minutes
Tumble-drier	40 minutes
Hand-held hair drier	40 minutes
Microwave oven	45 minutes
Turbo-type vacuum cleaner	50 minutes
Hot-water immersion heater	1 hour

Ordinary vacuum cleaner	1 hour 30 minutes
Large television	4 hours
100-W light bulb	10 hours
Small, portable television	12 hours
Small domestic music system	12 hours
Fluorescent low-energy light bulb	30 hours
Electric toothbrush	40–50 hours

A fuse is a very thin piece of wire, usually inside a small rod-shaped container. If a fault causes too much electricity to pass through it, the fuse gets too hot and easily melts, breaking the circuit.

Live, neutral and earth

Each circuit usually has three cables or wires. The live wire can be thought of as the one that carries electricity to a socket, light fitting, or electrical appliance. The neutral wire takes the electricity away again. The earth is a safety wire, which is connected through the earthing circuit to a metal rod in the ground. If electricity gets to something it should not get to – such as the metal case of an appliance – the earth wire carries this potentially lethal electricity safely into the ground. This prevents the case becoming 'live' and giving shocks.

FUTURE FILE

HOMES OF TOMORROW
The 'smart home' of the future may be more energy-efficient by monitoring conditions both inside and outside the house, and keeping very close control of electrical devices. For example, it may be able to detect changes in the weather, how many people are in the house, which rooms they are in, what activities they are doing and even what they are wearing. It would then adjust the heating and lighting to waste as little electricity as possible.

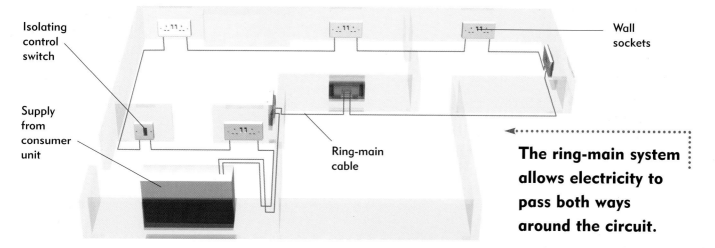

Isolating control switch

Supply from consumer unit

Ring-main cable

Wall sockets

The ring-main system allows electricity to pass both ways around the circuit.

Rings of cables

The circuits that take electricity to wall sockets, and often to lights, are called ring-mains. The cables come out of the consumer unit to the first socket, then to the next, and so on, and finally from the last socket back to the consumer unit. The result is a circle or ring of sockets joined by cables.

At certain times of day, such as when people come home from work and turn on lights and electrical appliances, demand for power in big cities increases greatly.

ELECTRICITY AND MAGNETISM IN MEDICINE

lectricity is part of life – and it can also save life. The body works by tiny, fast-moving electrical pulses called nerve signals. They flash along the network of nerves that connects the brain and spinal cord to the muscles and other body parts. Nerve signals carry information and instructions that control and regulate the body's functions and movements. Even the thoughts and ideas in our minds are electrical, made up of nerve signals in the brain itself. And as the heart and other muscles work, they too produce electrical pulses.

Sensors on the skin

These tiny electrical signals 'ripple' naturally through the body to the skin. They can be detected by sensors attached to the skin, then amplified in strength, and displayed as a pattern on a screen or paper chart. Doctors use such signal patterns to help identify illness and disease.

• The ECG (eletrocardiograph) machine measures electrical signals from the heart. It can show if the heart is beating too fast or too slow, if the heart muscle is weak, or if the heart has suffered a lack of blood, as in a heart attack.

Monitoring the heart using an ECG machine is completely painless.

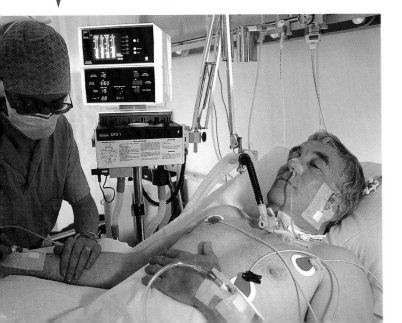

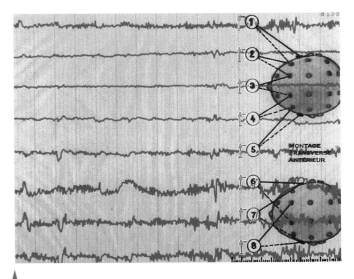

This print-out from an EEG machine records electrical signals in the brain.

• The EEG (electroencephalograph) machine measures electrical signals from the brain. It can show if the brain's activities have been affected by a condition such as epilepsy (fits) or stroke. The EEG can also monitor the brain's activity during sleep and show when we are dreaming.

• The EMG (electromyograph) machine measures electrical signals from muscles. It can help to identify or diagnose problems such as muscle weakness, wasting, trembling or paralysis.

• The GSR (galvanic skin response) machine measures how well the skin carries or conducts very small, harmless pulses of electricity. Nervous sweating affects this, which is why GSR is used in 'lie detector' machines.

Setting the pace

The heart's beating is controlled by tiny electrical signals, like nerve signals. In some conditions, the heart does not beat in a regular fashion, but becomes jerky and erratic. A pacemaker is a small electronic device put into the body, usually under the skin of the shoulder or abdomen, and connected to the heart by thin wires. It produces regular electrical signals that make the heart beat steadily again.

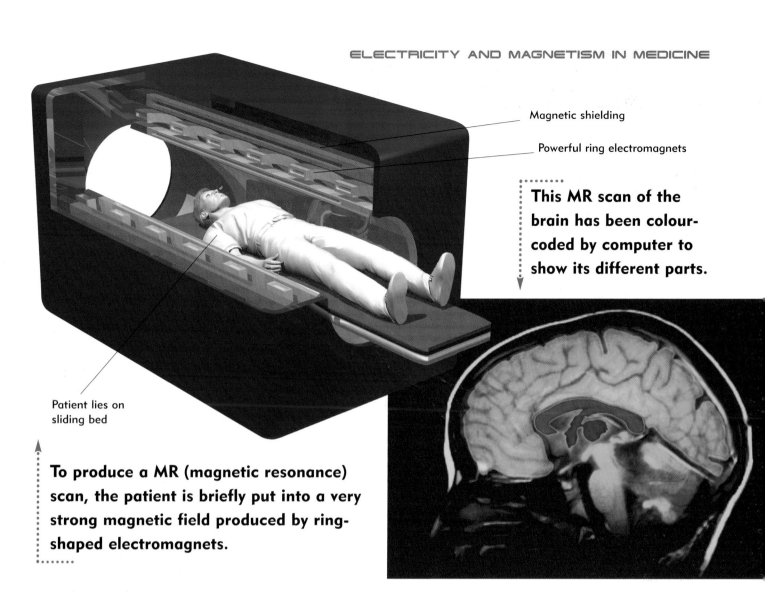

Magnetic shielding

Powerful ring electromagnets

Patient lies on sliding bed

This MR scan of the brain has been colour-coded by computer to show its different parts.

To produce a MR (magnetic resonance) scan, the patient is briefly put into a very strong magnetic field produced by ring-shaped electromagnets.

Shocked into life

In a heart attack, the heart may stop beating in its normal, regular, powerful way, and tremble or 'fibrillate'. In a cardiac arrest, the heart stops completely. This can be fatal within minutes. The defibrillator is an electrical machine with two large metal plates that are put on the patient's chest. Electric pulses sent between the plates pass through the heart. The electric shock is designed to jerk the heart back into a regular beat.

Electromagnetic pictures

Hospitals often use MRI (magnetic resonance imaging) scanners to see inside the body without resorting to exploratory surgery. The scanner puts the body in a powerful but harmless magnetic field and detects how its cells and tissues respond to weak pulses of radio waves. It produces accurate pictures of nerves, blood vessels and other delicate parts of the body.

HISTORY FILE

SHOCK TREATMENT

Some years ago, certain mental and behavioural problems were treated by ECT (electroconvulsive therapy). Large metal plates similar to those of a heart defibrillator machine (left) were put on the patient's head, and powerful electric currents passed through various parts of the brain. These made the patient's body stiffen, jerk, twitch and convulse. The hope was that the electric shocks would restore the brain's normal electrical nerve signals. ECT had very mixed effects and is hardly used today, except in a few cases for severe depression.

ELECTROMAGNETIC WAVES

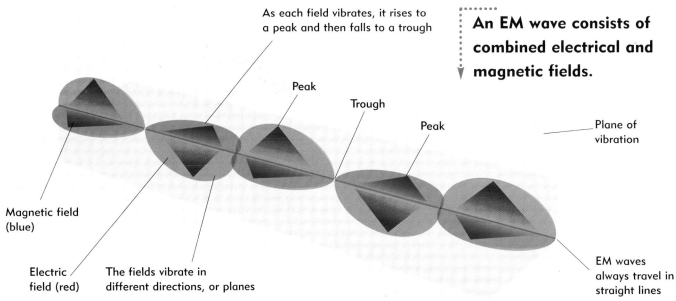

As each field vibrates, it rises to a peak and then falls to a trough

An EM wave consists of combined electrical and magnetic fields.

Peak

Trough

Peak

Plane of vibration

Magnetic field (blue)

Electric field (red)

The fields vibrate in different directions, or planes

EM waves always travel in straight lines

Electromagnetic (EM) waves are a form of energy. These energy waves consist of vibrating electrical and magnetic fields. They can pass through air, some liquids, even some solids, and also through the near-emptiness of deep space. EM waves travel faster than anything else in the Universe, at about 300,000 km per second. There are several types of EM waves, including light rays, radio waves, microwaves, and X-rays. They are the same type of EM energy, but they differ in their frequencies (the number of waves per second) and so also in their lengths. A radio wave may be more than 1 km long, while a microwave in a microwave oven is about 12 cm long. A light wave is so short that it takes many thousands to make up just 1 mm. Together, the whole range of different types of electromagnetic waves is known as the electromagnetic spectrum.

Waves for seeing

Light, as we know, is vitally important to us, because it enables us to see and understand the world around us. Light is especially useful in machines when it is in a very pure, intense, powerful form known as laser light. Beams of laser light are used to carry out delicate eye surgery, to play compact discs (CDs) in music systems and read CDs in computers, to send information through the telephone system as flashes of light along optical fibres, and even to cut through thick metal sheets in industry.

FACT FILE

ELECTROMAGNETIC WAVELENGTHS
These are the numbers of the different types of EM waves that would fit into 10 centimetres – about the same as the distance across the palm of an average adult hand. This gives an idea of just how much these waves vary in length, although they are all the same form of EM energy.

Radio waves: from less than one-thousandth of a wave, to about half a wave.
Microwaves: from about one-tenth of one wave, to 10 waves.
Infrared (heat) rays: about 100 to 10,000 waves.
Light rays: about 100,000 to 1 million (1,000,000) waves.
Ultraviolet rays: about 10 million to 100 million waves.
X-rays: around 1 billion (1,000 million) waves.
Gamma rays: 100 billion or more waves.

Waves for broadcasting

Radio and television stations send out, or broadcast, their programmes from transmitter masts, dishes, or satellites using radio waves. During broadcasting, the waves' height, or amplitude, and frequency are varied, or modulated. The patterns of these variations carry coded information about a programme's sounds and pictures. A television or radio aerial can pick up these waves and translate them back into sounds and pictures. Much weaker radio waves are used by mobile phones.

Satellite dishes are used to detect and transmit radio waves and microwaves.

Waves for cooking

Microwaves have a heating effect and are used to warm drinks and cook food in microwave ovens. The microwaves cook food by transferring their energy to water molecules inside the food. They can also, like radio waves, be modulated to carry information. Microwave transmitters and receivers form part of the telephone network, beaming signals between communications towers 40–50 km apart. Microwave signals can also be sent up to a satellite and back down again, to control the satellite's activities and receive information.

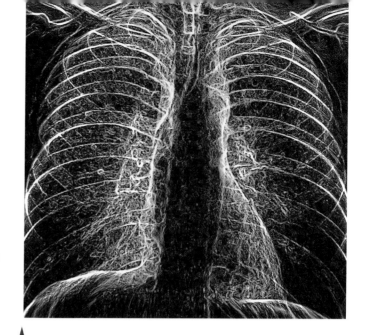

A chest X-ray is made with EM waves.

Waves for health

Doctors often use X-ray photographs to examine their patients. An X-ray photograph records how a beam of X-rays passes through the body. The rays are blocked by denser body parts, such as bones, teeth, and some organs, which show up on the photograph as light areas on a dark background. A computerized tomography (CT) scanner passes very weak X-rays through the body at different angles. A computer analyses the way the X-rays are absorbed, and uses this information to build up pictures of layers or 'slices' through the body. In radiotherapy, narrow beams of powerful X-rays are directed at abnormal growths on or in the body. The aim is to kill the cells and tissues of the growth, while leaving healthy parts unaffected.

Laser eye-surgery uses concentrated light beams to make delicate cuts in the eye.

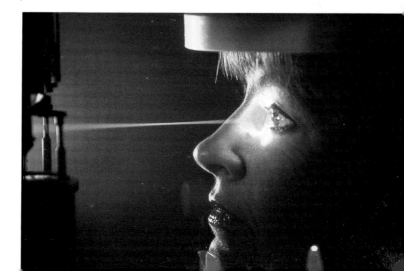

ELECTRONICS

Machines such as computers, video games, calculators, televisions and radios all rely on components that control, change, and manipulate small amounts of electric current. Using components in this way is called electronics.

Inside every electronic machine, tiny electric currents flowing through circuits are switched on and off or varied in strength. The currents are electrical signals that tell the machine to carry out specific tasks, such as adding up numbers in a calculator or word-processing in a computer. The circuits use a number of components to do this, including resistors, capacitors, diodes, and transistors. The components are often made of semiconducting materials such as silicon and germanium.

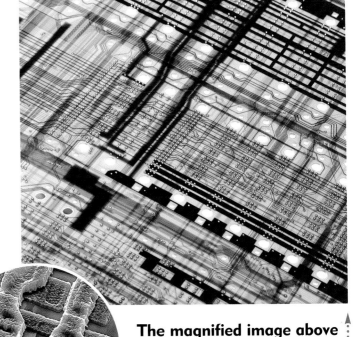

The magnified image above shows the maze of circuits and components on a microchip. Each is made of layers of semiconductors (left).

Microchips

Today, components can be made small enough to fit on a tiny 'microchip', a wafer-thin slice of silicon just a few millimetres square. The microchip may contain thousands of different components, all linked together or integrated, which is why microchips are also called integrated circuits. The components on the chip are made by laying different combinations of semiconductors and other materials on to the silicon wafer. Each different combination produces a different component. Microchips have allowed electronic devices to become smaller and cheaper.

Analogue and digital

The signals handled by electronic circuits are either analogue or digital. Analogue signals consist of constantly varying electric currents, such as the signals that operate a TV screen. Digital signals, such as those used in a calculator or computer, are made up of thousands of on-off pulses of current every second.

FUTURE FILE

CYBER-BODIES

Where will the science of electricity and magnetism – especially electronics – take us in the future? Here are some possibilities:

• Microchips could be put into the eye to receive light rays or into the ear to detect sound waves, helping people to see and hear more clearly.

• A tiny electronic thought-processor fixed to the head could detect the brain's electrical signals and transmit thoughts by radio waves directly to a computer.

• A whole human cyber-body could be constructed from advanced plastics and composites, using electric micro-motors, magnetic controls and ultra-microchip information processors. Simply connect your brain into the head, and you can live for ever!

Electronics in the modern world

The modern world is dominated by electronic devices. They allow information to flash around the planet almost instantly over the global computer network known as the Internet. In fact, almost all our communications rely on electronics, from radios and televisions, to telephones and faxes. The electronic computer is now essential in almost every industry, from writing books and designing clothes, to building cars and launching satellites. Electronic components are also at the heart of many life-saving machines in hospitals. They are also used in more everyday ways, such as the microchips that control washing machines, food processors and video players, and so much more. Electronics is here to stay!

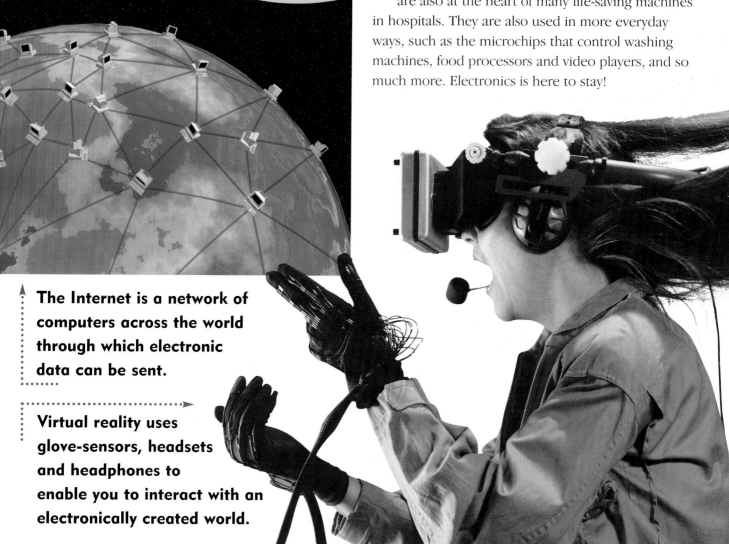

The Internet is a network of computers across the world through which electronic data can be sent.

Virtual reality uses glove-sensors, headsets and headphones to enable you to interact with an electronically created world.

GLOSSARY

Alternating current (AC) Electricity that repeatedly changes the direction in which it flows.

Atom Tiny particles from which everything is made.

Charge An amount of electricity.

Circuit The path around which electric current flows.

Conductors Materials that allow electricity to pass through them.

Direct current (DC) Electricity that flows around a circuit in one direction only.

Domain A tiny region of magnetism in an object.

Electric current A flow of electrons around a circuit.

Electric motor A device that changes electrical energy into movement.

Electrical cell A device that uses chemistry to produce electricity. Several linked cells form a battery.

Electrodes Parts of an electrical device that either give out or collect electrons.

Electrolysis A process that uses electricity to split up a substance.

Electrolyte A substance made up of ions that conducts electricity when it is molten or in solution.

Electromagnetic induction When a magnetic field causes a current to flow through a conductor.

Electromagnetic waves Energy in the form of electric and magnetic fields that travel as waves.

Electromotive force (emf) The pushing force that makes a current flow around a circuit.

Electrons Negatively-charged particles inside atoms.

Electrostatic induction When an electric charge on one object produces an electric charge on another.

Generator A device that converts the energy of movement into electricity.

Insulators Materials that do not conduct electricity.

Ions Atoms that have either lost or gained electrons.

Magnetic field The area around a magnet in which it exerts its force.

Nuclear reactions When atomic nuclei split apart or join together, releasing vast amounts of energy.

Nucleus (plural: nuclei) The centre of an atom.

Resistance When a substance opposes the flow of an electric current through it.

Semiconductors Materials that conduct electricity only under certain conditions.

Static discharge A sudden rush of electric charge.

Static electricity A build up of charge in one place.

FURTHER INFO

PLACES TO VISIT

Science Museum, Exhibition Road, South Kensington, London SW7 2DD, UK. Tel. 020 942 4000. Has a permanent display on electricity and magnetism.

Royal Institution, Albermarle Street, London W1X 4BS, UK. Tel. 020 409 2992. Find out more about electricity and magnetism from the world-renowned Royal Institution.

Museum of the History of Science, University of Oxford, Broad Street, Oxford OX1 3AZ, UK. Tel. 01865 271280. Information and displays on the history of science.

BOOKS TO READ

Electricity and Magnetism by Margaret Walley and Jason Page (book and PC disc, Two-Can Publishing, 1998)

Eyewitness Science: Electricity by Steve Parker (Dorling Kindersley, 1998)

Fact Finders: Electricity and Magnetism by Mike Clemmet and Terry Kennett (BBC Publishing, 1997)

Learn About Magnets by Steve Parker (Lorenz Books/Anness Publishing, 1996)

Science Workshop: Electricity by Pam Robson (Watts/Shooting Star Press, 1997)

Science Workshop: Magnetism by Pam Robson (Watts/Shooting Star Press, 1997)

Shocking Science! (book and experiment kit, Sterling Publishing, 1999)

WEB SITES

http://www.nmsi.ac.uk/Welcome.html
Science Museum web site, with online exhibitions, views of the collections and news of special events.

http://www.ri.ac.uk
Researcher's homepage for the Royal Institution.

http://www.mhs.ox.ac.uk
Web site of the Museum of the History of Science.

http://kidscience.tqn.com/msub26.htm
Site containing science links for kids, including many on electricity and energy.

INDEX

The Earth's Magnetic Field

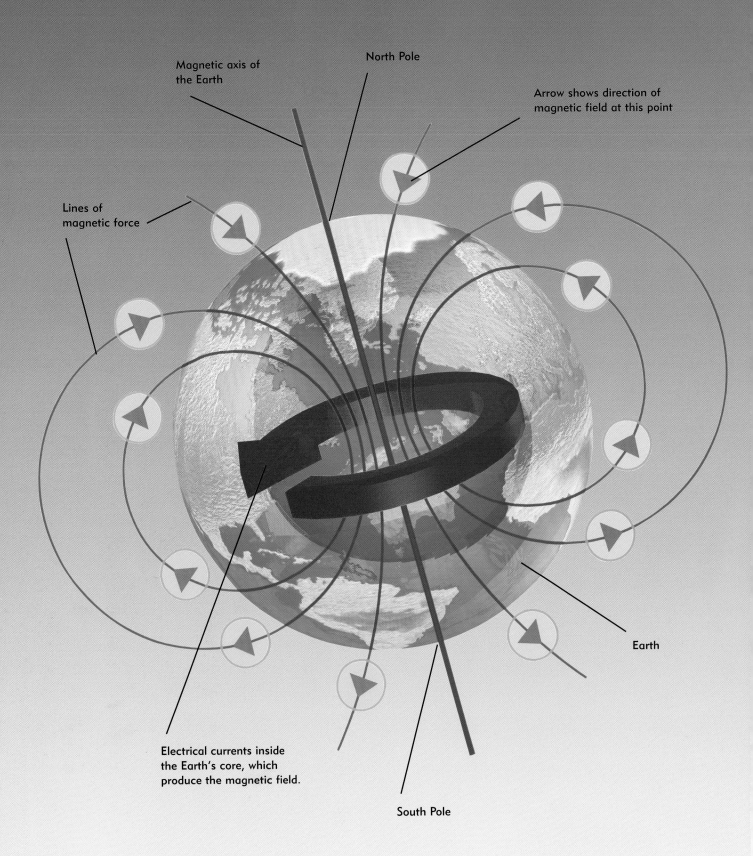

Magnetic axis of the Earth

North Pole

Arrow shows direction of magnetic field at this point

Lines of magnetic force

Earth

Electrical currents inside the Earth's core, which produce the magnetic field.

South Pole

ELECTRICITY AND MAGNETISM – Quantities and units

Basic quantities

Quantity	Symbol	Basic SI unit	Abbreviation
Length	l	metre	m
Time	t	second	s
Current	I	ampere	A

Derived quantities (these are based on those above)

Quantity	Symbol	Equation or definition	Unit name and abbreviation	Derived SI unit
Power	P	energy transferred ÷ time	watt (W)	$J\ s^{-1}$
Electric charge	Q	current x time	coulomb (C)	$A\ s$
Potential difference or electromotive force	V	energy transferred ÷ charge	volt (V)	$J\ C^{-1}$
Capacitance	C	charge ÷ potential difference	farad (F)	$C\ V^{-1}$
Resistance	R	potential difference ÷ current	ohm (Ω)	$V\ A^{-1}$
Conductance	G	energy transferred ÷ time	siemens (S)	$J\ s^{-1}$
Electric flux density	D	charge ÷ area	coulomb/metre^2	$C\ m^{-2}$
Electric field strength	E	potential difference ÷ distance	volt/metre	$V\ m^{-1}$
Magnetic flux	Φ	electromotive force x time	weber (Wb)	$V\ s$
Magnetic flux density	B	magnetic flux ÷ area	tesla (T)	$Wb\ m^{-2}$
Magnetic field strength	H	current ÷ distance	ampere/metre	$A\ m^{-1}$